P9-ECN-942

Track and Field

BY M. K. OSBORNE

AMICUS | AMICUS INK

Amicus High Interest is published by Amicus and Amicus Ink
P.O. Box 1329, Mankato, MN 56002
www.amicuspublishing.us

Library of Congress Cataloging-in-Publication Data
Names: Osborne, M. K., author.
Title: Track and field / by M.K. Osborne.
Description: Mankato, Minnesota : Amicus | Amicus Ink, [2020] | Series: Summer Olympic sports | Audience: Grades: 4 to 6. | Includes webography. | Includes index.
Identifiers: LCCN 2019005681 (print) | LCCN 2019009480 (ebook) | ISBN 9781681518657 (pdf) | ISBN 9781681518251 (library binding) | ISBN 9781681525532(paperback)
Subjects: LCSH: Track and field–Juvenile literature. | Olympics–Juvenile literature.
Classification: LCC GV1060.55 (ebook) | LCC GV1060.55 .O86 2020 (print) | DDC 796.42–dc23
LC record available at https://lccn.loc.gov/2019005681

Editor: Wendy Dieker
Designer: Aubrey Harper
Photo Researcher: Shane Freed

Photo Credits: Andrew Medichini/AP cover; Kyodo News/Newscom 4, 24–25; PCN Black/Alamy 7, 12, 27; Adrian Dennis/Getty 8; Fabrice Coffrini/Getty 10–11; David Davies/Alamy 15; Matt Dunham/AP 16, 19; David J. Phillip/AP 20; Xinhua/SIPA/Newscom 23; PCN Photography/Alamy 27; Xinhua/Alamy 28

Printed in the United States of America

HC 10 9 8 7 6 5 4 3 2 1
PB 10 9 8 7 6 5 4 3 2 1

Table of Contents

The Olympic 200-meter dash features the fastest women in the world.

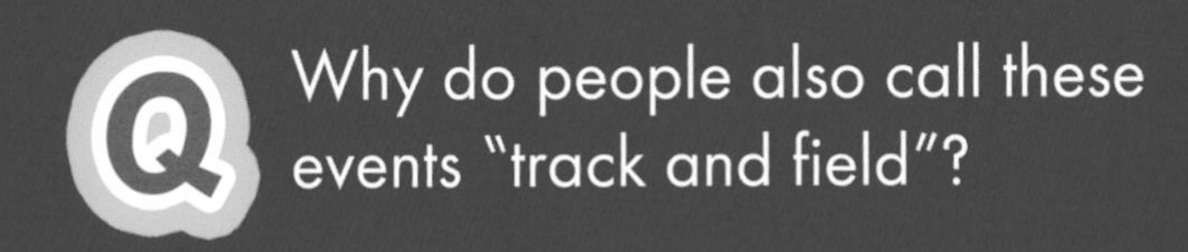

Why do people also call these events "track and field"?

Athletic Greatness

On your marks! Get set! Go! It's time for track and field at the Olympic Games. Some people call these events "athletics." That's because these events are true shows of athletic greatness. Athletes from around the world come to the Olympics to run, jump, and throw. Who will win a gold medal?

The running events take place on a big oval track. Throwing and jumping events take place on a grassy field.

Running Events

Bang! The starting gun fires. **Sprinters** bolt off the line with blazing speed in short races. The shortest race is the 100-meter dash. The winner often crosses the finish line in less than 10 seconds! Sprinters also run in 200-meter and 400-meter races. Don't blink! Winners can cross the finish line a hundredth of a second before the rest of the runners.

Gold medalist Usain Bolt takes off in the 100-meter dash. He is called the greatest sprinter of all time.

JAMAICA
Rio2016
BOLT
Rio2016
6
MONDO

U.S. gold medalist English Gardner takes the baton to start her part of the 4x100 race.

How many meters long is the Olympic track?

In the **relay** races, teams of four runners each take a turn racing around the track. The first runner sprints and hands a baton to the next runner. The first team to carry the baton across the finish line wins. You will see two different relay races. In the 4x100, each runner goes 100 meters. In the 4x400, each runner goes once around the track.

It is 400 meters all the way around.

Another fast race event is the **hurdles**. Runners speed down their lanes. As they run, they leap over the hurdles. One missed jump can send a runner crashing down to the track! With such short races, a fall will cost the race. Only the strongest and fastest runners are Olympic hurdlers.

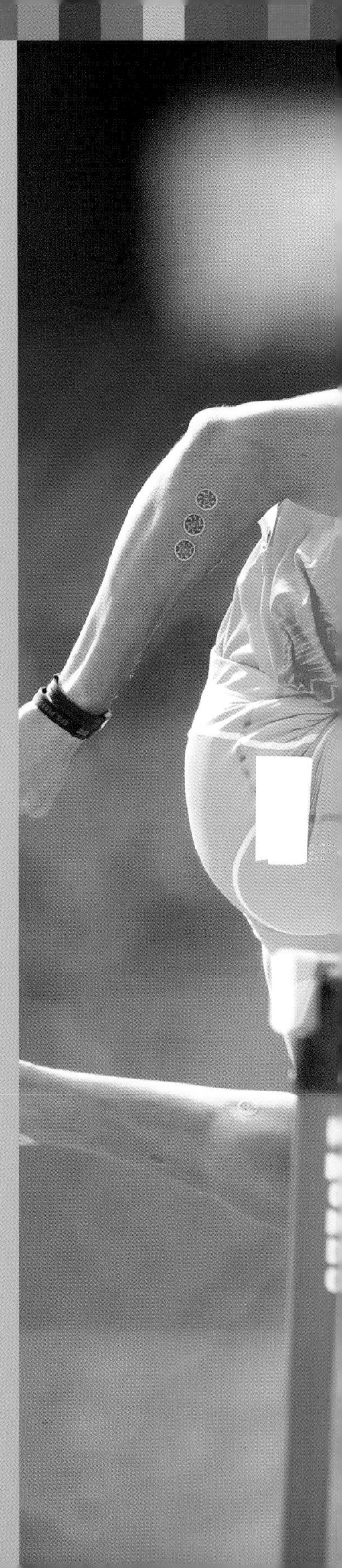

Keisuke Ushiro of Japan hops over a hurdle at the 2016 Olympics.

Rio2016
Rio2016
MONDO

U.S. distance runner Lopez Lomong leads the group in the 5,000-meter race.

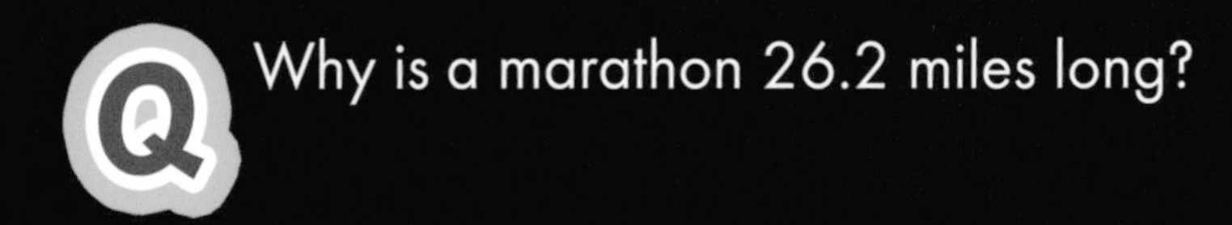

Why is a marathon 26.2 miles long?

Some races are not quite as fast. Long-distance runners compete in races from 800 meters to 10,000 meters. The longest race is the marathon. It is 26.2 miles (42.2 km) long! For these races, runners need to run fast enough to keep up. But they can't run too fast. They might be too tired by the end.

The race comes from an old Greek story about a soldier who ran about 26 miles (42 km) from Marathon to Athens.

Jumping Events

One exciting jumping event is the long jump. It starts with a sprint down the runway. Jumpers launch off the board. Sand flies as they land in the pit. The longest jump wins.

In the triple jump, athletes run and then string three jumps together. The total distance of the jumps is measured.

British long jumper Greg Rutherford leaps to win a bronze medal in 2016.

London 2012
RUTHERFORD

Swedish high jumper Emma Green does the Fosbury flop in the 2012 Olympics.

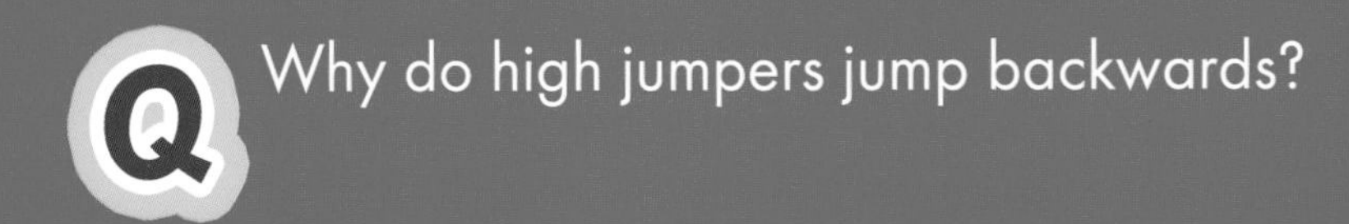

Why do high jumpers jump backwards?

High jumpers are looking for height. These athletes jump over a bar. The bar gets higher and higher with each jump. Each jumper's score is the highest bar they can jump over. How high can they jump? The best usually get higher than 6.5 feet (2 meters)!

High jumpers used to leap like hurdlers. In 1968, Dick Fosbury jumped headfirst. He easily won. Soon all high jumpers were doing the "Fosbury flop."

If you think the high jump is amazing, head over to the pole vault. Vaulters start by running with a long pole toward a high bar. They plant the pole in a "box" at the end of the track. The pole launches the vaulter up to the bar. They arch their backs and toss themselves over the bar. Like the high jump, the pole vault bar gets higher as vaulters make it over.

How high does the pole vaulting bar get?

Canada's Damian Warner easily clears the pole vault bar.

The Olympic record for men is 19.8 feet (6.03 meters). That means a pole vaulter could fly right over an adult giraffe!

Ukraine's Oleksandr Pyatnytsya can throw a javelin nearly the length of a football field.

Throwing Events

The Olympic throwing events are shows of strength. Fans see four kinds of events. In one event, athletes hurl a spear called a javelin. They run down a track and then throw the spear as far as they can. The farthest throw wins. The finalists throw farther than 187 feet (57 m).

Other athletes hurl a heavy disc down the field. Discus throwers spin in a tight circle. Then they whip their arm around to throw the discus.

Another test of strength is the hammer throw. The "hammer" is actually a heavy ball on a long wire. Throwers spin around, holding onto the end of the wire. Finally they let go and the hammer whizzes through the air. The thrower with the longest distance wins.

Gold medalist Christoph Harting of Germany spins around before letting the discus fly.

USA
Rio2016
CARTER

Heave! The **shot put** event is about pure strength. Like other throwers, shot putters start by spinning around. Then they chuck the heavy, round shot as far as they can. It's not like throwing a baseball, though. A men's shot weighs just over 16 pounds (7.26 kg). That's almost 50 times heavier than a baseball!

Gold medalist Michelle Carter of the U.S. winds up to throw the heavy shot.

The Greatest Athletes

The Olympic motto is "Faster, higher, stronger." Since ancient times, athletes have tried to run the fastest, jump the highest, and be the strongest. Today, the men's **decathlon** challenges athletes in ten different track and field events. The women compete in seven events in the **heptathlon**. Some call the winners the world's greatest athletes.

British gold medalist Jessica Ennis-Hill celebrates a win during the 2012 Olympic heptathlon.

The three fastest men accept medals for the 100-meter dash in the 2016 Olympics.

There's a lot going on in the track and field stadium. The races are fast. The jumps are high. The throws are strong. Athletes train hard to be the best. They all want the highest prize: a gold medal. Cheer on your country's top stars at the Summer Olympics.

Glossary

baton A short stick handed from one runner to another during a relay race.

decathlon The men's all-around track and field competition that includes ten events.

heptathlon The women's all-around track and field competition that includes seven events.

hurdles A sprint race with small fences set up on the track for runners to leap over.

javelin A spear used in throwing events.

relay A race that a team of people do; each runner takes a turn running part of the race.

shot put An event where an athlete throws a heavy steel ball as far as possible.

sprinter A runner who specializes in running very fast over a short distance.

Read More

Amstutz, Lisa J. *The Science Behind Track and Field.* Mankato, Minn.: Capstone Press, 2016.

Herman, Gail. *What Are the Summer Olympics?* New York: Penguin Random House, 2016.

Kortemeier, Todd. *12 Reasons to Love Track and Field.* Mankato, Minn.: 12 Story Library, 2018.

Websites

Athletics | Olympic.org
www.olympic.org/athletics

Track and Field | NBC Olympics
http://nbcolympics.com/sport/track-and-field/

USA Track and Field
http://www.usatf.org/Sports/Track---Field.aspx

Every effort has been made to ensure that these websites are appropriate for children. However, because of the nature of the Internet, it is impossible to guarantee that these sites will remain active indefinitely or that their contents will not be altered.

Index

About the Author

M. K. Osborne is a children's writer and editor who gets excited about the Olympics, both the Summer and Winter Games, every two years. Osborne pores over stats and figures and medal counts to bring the best stories about the Olympics to young readers.